Face to Face

DINOSAURS

Q2AMedia

Created by Q2AMedia
www.q2amedia.com
Text, design & illustrations Copyright © 2008 Q2AMedia

Editor Honor Head
Publishing Director Chester Fisher
Creative Director Simmi Sikka
Senior Designers Joita Das and Ravijot Singh

Illustrators Subhash Vohra, Aadil A Siddiqui, and Amit Tayal
Art Editor Sujatha Menon
Picture Researcher Lalit Dalal

an imprint of
SCHOLASTIC
www.scholastic.com

Scholastic and Tangerine Press and associated logos are trademarks of Scholastic Inc.

Published by Tangerine Press, an imprint of Scholastic Inc., 557 Broadway; New York, NY 10012

Scholastic Canada Ltd.
Markham, Ontario

Scholastic Australia Pty. Ltd.
Gosford NSW

Scholastic New Zealand Ltd
Greenmount, Auckland

Scholastic UK
Coventry, Warwickshire

Grolier International, Inc.
Makati City, Philippines

10 9 8 7 6 5 4 3 2 1

ISBN-10: 0-545-06322-1
ISBN-13: 978-0-545-06322-7

Printed in China

Picture Credits

Cover Images:
Front Q2AMedia
Back Highlights for Children: Oxford Scientific Films: Photolibrary
Half Title Highlights for Children: Oxford Scientific Films: Photolibrary & Scott Sanders

6 Reconstruction by Michael Rothman. **8** Natural History Museum, London. **10-11** John Sibbick. **11t** Highlights for Children: Oxford Scientific Films: Photolibrary. **11b** The Natural History Museum, London. **12-13** Todd Marshall. **13t** Todd Marshall. **13b** Emily Willoughby. **16** Todd Marshall. **17t** Illustration ©2007 John Bindon. **17b** Courtesy of The Mongolian Museum of Natural History. **18b** Julius T. Csotonyi. **20-21** Mauricio Anton: SPL: Photolibrary. **21t** Todd Marshall. **22t** Reconstruction by Michael Rothman. **22-23** Illustration ©2007 John Bindon. **26-27** Illustration ©2007 John Bindon. **27t** Lynton Gardiner ©Dorling Kindersley, Courtesy of The American Museum of Natural History. **28-29** Todd Marshall. **29t** The Natural History Museum, London. **31t** Anness Publishing: Practical Pictures. **32-33** Illustration ©2007 John Bindon. **33t** The Natural History Museum, London. **34b** Artwork Copyright Joe Tucciarone: Science Photo Library: Photolibrary. **35** Photo Researchers, Inc: Photolibrary. **36** Miles Kelly: Fotolibra. **37t** Illustration ©2007 John Bindon. **37b** Highlights for Children: Oxford Scientific Films: Photolibrary. **38-39** Illustration ©2007 John Bindon. **40-41** Illustrations ©2007 John Bindon. **42t** Todd Marshall **42-43** The Natural History Museum, London. **44-45bm & br** Ezequiel Vera.

Face to Face

DINOSAURS

Dougal Dixon

tangerine Press
an imprint of
SCHOLASTIC
www.scholastic.com

Contents

Centrosaurus

Tyrannosaurus rex

Armor in Action 30

Plant-eaters such as the *Ankylosaurus* and *Edmontonia* could do terrible damage with their armor of deadly spikes, clubbed tails, and sheets of bony plates. They used these weapons against each other as well as to defend themselves from the fierce meat-eaters.

The Tiny Dinos 34

Meet some of the smallest and strangest looking of the dinosaurs. These tiny creatures such as the *Compsognathus* were sometimes no bigger than a chicken. Many, including the *Microraptor,* were feathered.

The Dinosaur's World 38

Snarling mammals the size of badgers, snaggle-toothed flying reptiles, and monstrous sea lizards all shared the dinosaur's world.

Timeline and Record Breakers 44

At-a-glance look at which dinosaurs lived in which period, plus some fascinating facts.

Dinosaur Words 46

Index 48

Discovering Dinosaurs

The dinosaurs were amazing animals that existed for about 160 million years. The timeline on pages 44-45 shows which dinosaurs lived during the different time periods.

In the beginning

When the first dinosaurs appeared toward the end of the Triassic period, all of Earth's landmasses were joined together in one supercontinent called Pangaea.

The earth was made up of hot desert areas and oceans. Dinosaurs developed from small, lizardlike animals. At first, the same types of dinosaurs were found all over the world, mostly near the sea.

Dinosaur domination

In the Jurassic period, the continents had begun to split apart. Shallow seaways separated huge areas of land from others. The climate became milder and moister. Dinosaurs dominated the land from the ocean's edge to the thick, dark forests far from the sea.

North America

Asia

Africa

South America

▲ **Cretaceous world**
144-65 million years ago

Different dinosaurs

By the end of the Cretaceous period, most of the individual continents were separate from one another. There were different types of dinosaurs in different parts of the world, such as North America, Africa, South America, and Asia.

◀ *Even before the dinosaurs appeared, the world was full of big reptiles. A Texas riverside 280 million years ago might have looked like this.*

▲ **Jurassic world**
213-144 million years ago

Pangaea

▼ **Triassic world**
248-213 million years ago

The Meat-Eaters

Some of the biggest and mightiest animals that ever lived were the huge meat-eating dinosaurs, and none were greater than *Tyrannosaurus rex*.

King of the killers

Tyrannosaurus rex was perhaps the most powerful meat-eater that ever lived. It was about 40 feet (12 m) long and stood 10 feet (3 m) at the hips. It weighed more than 7 tons (7 tonnes). *Tyrannosaurus rex* had up to 50 teeth in its mouth at a time. It was the fiercest flesh-shearing, bone-crunching animal of its time.

▼ Tyrannosaurus *used its powerful legs to charge at its prey with great speed. Its feet had heavy, blunt nails, almost like hooves, to carry the weight of its body.*

The shape of the killer

Like all meat-eating dinosaurs, *Tyrannosaurus* had a small body for its size. It stood and ran with its backbone held straight horizontally, its head and teeth out at the front, and its heavy tail straight out at the back for balance. *Tyrannosaurus* held its head in an S-shape, ready for action. Replacement teeth grew deep in its jaws to take the place of any teeth that wore down or broke off during an attack.

Short front arms were probably not used for hunting.

Eyes point forward to judge the distance to its prey.

Short, thick, strong front teeth used for gripping struggling animals.

Side teeth were bladelike for shearing meat off the bone.

A killing bite

Tyrannosaurus probably hunted by ambush. It would have waited until a big plant-eater like a duckbill came by, and then burst out of the undergrowth at 25 mph (40 kph). It slammed its massive jaws into the back and flanks of its prey and killing it with powerful bites.

Tyrannosaurus would bite into its prey with its powerful jaws. Then it used its great strength to pull the victim to the ground.

Jaws and teeth

Although *Tyrannosaurus* only used its jaws to kill its prey, other big meat-eaters used their claws as well. *Allosaurus,* from late Jurassic North America, had three-fingered hands that would have been big enough to grasp your head one-handed! The thumb was flexible and had an enormous and very sharp ripping claw.

The claw of the Allosaurus *was big enough to slice through the skin of a big plant-eater and slash blood vessels.*

Scavengers

It may be that some of the biggest meat-eaters were scavengers rather than hunters–eating the meat from animals that had already died. Some experts think that *Tyrannosaurus* lived like this. The meat-eater *Megalosaurus* probably scavenged dead animals from the shoreline.

Fossils of Megalosaurus *found in France lie in rocks left in shallow sea water. The animals died as they prowled along the beaches looking for prey.*

FACT

Tyrannosaurus tooth-marks have been found on the fossilized hip bones and head shields of the horned dinosaur *Triceratops.*

The biggest of all

Giganotosaurus was the longest known meat-eating dinosaur at 45 feet (13½ m). It lived in the late Cretaceous period in South America, where it preyed upon the biggest of the long-necked plant-eaters, such as *Argentinosaurus*.

We can tell what dinosaurs ate by looking at fossil dung, called coprolite. *Tyrannosaurus* coprolite shows fragments of dinosaur bone from a duckbill.

FACT

 Giganotosaurus *was longer* than Tyrannosaurus *but may not have been as heavy.*

⏶ *A pack of* Giganotosaurus *could easily overpower a huge plant-eater such as this* Argentinosaurus.

Hunting in packs

The medium-sized meat-eaters, like *Ceratosaurus*, may have caught the biggest plant-eaters of the time by hunting in packs, like wolves do today. They surrounded their prey and then attacked.

Fish-eaters

Not all carnivorous dinosaurs hunted and ate other dinosaurs. *Suchomimus* was a fish-eater that lived in Africa. It had a long claw on its thumb that it used for hooking fish out of shallow streams. Its close relative, the *Baryonyx* which roamed in Europe, has been found with fish scales in its stomach. *Masiakasaurus* was another fish-eater and had long, spiky teeth in the front of its jaws. These would have been ideal for grabbing small, slippery prey, like fish.

⏷ Suchomimus *had a head like that of a crocodile. Its name means "crocodile mimic."*

Small and Deadly

Some of the most ferocious dinosaurs were small carnivores (meat-eaters). With their slashing claws and razor-sharp teeth, they were swift hunters. A pack could bring down a much bigger dinosaur.

Killer claw

The deadly weapon of some smaller meat-eating dinosaurs, such as *Deinonychus*, was a retractable claw like that of a cat. This enormous claw was held out of the way when the animal walked, but could be brought down with a slashing action when it attacked another dinosaur. It was razor-sharp and strong enough to seriously harm a huge enemy.

◀ *The killer sickle claw could be used with a swift and deadly swipe. This large claw was one of three on each hind foot.*

A pack of trouble

Deinonychus hunted in packs. Scientists have found the remains of several of them scattered around the body of a much larger animal. They would have hurled themselves at the victim, forcing it to the ground before eating its flesh.

Big brain used to coordinate an attack.

Rows of extremely sharp teeth.

Jaws worked back and forth in a sawlike motion.

Stiff, straight tail helped the dinosaur to balance.

Three clawed, grasping fingers.

Killing claw on the hind foot.

A feathered fury

Hissing, spitting, slashing, and flinging itself at its prey, the turkey-sized *Velociraptor* was one of the most vicious of the small and deadly dinosaurs. With killing claws on its hands and feet, and a mouth full of daggerlike teeth, nothing could escape its attack.

▼ *Experts found a Velociraptor skeleton wrapped around that of the horned dinosaur Protoceratops. Their fight was so violent it killed them both.*

Food for the family

Troodon was more lightweight than *Velociraptor* or *Deinonychus*, but it still had the killing claw on its foot. Nesting sites show that it brought back dead, plant-eating dinosaurs to feed its growing young. The smallest of the sickle-clawed hunters was the goose-sized *Bambiraptor*, which hunted in the undergrowth, killing and eating small animals.

▲ Troodon *chicks were fed the corpses of plant-eating dinosaurs, which were dragged back to the nest by the parents.*

Death in the sand

A number of skeletons found in the Mongolian desert show how *Velociraptor* used its hind foot when attacking a *Protoceratops*. It pushed its claw deep into the innards of the *Protoceratops* to cause a deadly wound. The *Protoceratops* tried to defended itself by seizing the arm of the *Velociraptor* in its beak. In this fight, both dinosaurs died when a sand dune collapsed and buried them.

▶| *Frozen in time, the skeletons of* Velociraptor *and* Protoceratops *lie in the position in which they died 80 million years ago.*

Dinosaur Giants

The biggest of the dinosaurs was a group called the sauropods—the long-necked plant-eaters. They were the biggest of any land animals that have ever existed.

◄ *Plant-eaters such as Diplodocus had stones that gathered in a part of their stomach called the crop.*

Constant feeding

The enormous *Brachiosaurus* was one of the tallest of all the dinosaurs, standing more than 50 feet (15 m) high. It had to eat all the time to take in enough food to keep its huge body going.

Stomach full of stones

A sauropod did not have time to chew between breaking off and swallowing huge mouthfuls of greenery. Instead, sauropods swallowed stones to help grind down the plant material that made up their diet. Modern plant-eating birds like pheasants and chickens swallow grit for this reason, as they cannot chew with their beaks. The plant-eating dinosaurs swallowed stones the size of golf balls.

The eyes were at the sides of the head, so the dinosaur would see danger coming from all directions.

Large nostrils were at the top of the head. This may have been to keep the brain cool.

The teeth were used to comb leaves and twigs from the branches. There were no teeth for chewing.

Broad jaws meant that big mouthfuls of food could be taken.

Standing still

The sauropods lived at a time when there were huge forests with thick, towering tress that provided all the food these enormous beasts needed. A sauropod used its long, flexible neck to reach the top of the trees, or to search for fresh vegetation. It did not need to move its whole body to reach food.

▼ *Despite their enormous size, sauropods such as this Saltasaurus laid small eggs. The largest sauropod eggs known were only about 11 inches (30 cm) long.*

Short-neck, long-neck

Brachytrachelopan was an unusual plant-eater with a short neck! Experts believe it fed on plants growing very close to the ground. Despite that, it was closely related to *Diplodocus,* which had one of the longest necks of all the sauropods.

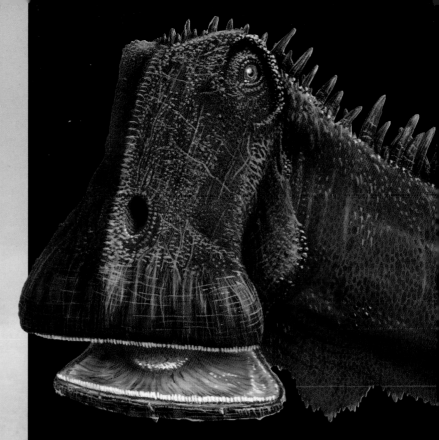

Vacuum-mouth

Some of the sauropods, like *Nigersaurus,* had very broad, straight-fronted mouths, like the broad nozzle of a vacuum cleaner. It used its mouth to "vacuum" up as much food as possible from the ground.

Two-footed plant-eaters

The other major plant-eating dinosaur group, ornithopods, became important during the Cretaceous period, after the sauropods. Ornithopods moved their entire body, rather than just their necks, to find food. They lived in swampy mud flats. *Iguanodon* was a typical ornithopod. As a youngster it scampered around on its hind legs, but when it became an adult, it was too heavy and had to walk on all fours.

◄ *Iguanodon was the first plant-eating dinosaur to be discovered.*

Teeth for chewing

Unlike the sauropods, the ornithopods could chew their food. They had crushing and grinding teeth as well as jaws that worked with a chewing action. While the food was chewed, it was held in their special cheek pouches as it was prepared for digestion. These dinosaurs did not need stomach stones to grind their food.

Last of the giants

The main plant-eaters at the end of the age of the dinosaurs were the duckbills. These had thick beaks. Many of them had strange crests on their heads that helped to distinguish one herd from another. The crests also were used for making noises to communicate through the swamps and forests.

▼ *Herds of duckbills, such as* Edmontosaurus, *took over from the sauropods as the main herbivores in Cretaceous times.*

FACT

A duckbill had dozens of grinding teeth in its jaws, packed together. These formed a continuous grinding surface, and were constantly replaced as they wore out.

Horns, Frills, and Spikes

Huge head frills, sharp horns, and long body spikes made up the deadly armor of many plant-eating dinosaurs.

Hornheads

Achelousaurus was one of the ceratopsians, or horned dinosaurs. These plant-eaters had big, rhinoceroslike bodies and looked very similar to one another. The only way to tell the species apart was to look at the arrangement of the horns on the head.

▶| Styracosaurus *had a single horn on the nose, which was used to rip open the belly of a bigger enemy.*

Big-head

The ceratopsian's head was a solid mass of armor. It had a shield or a frill on its back to protect its neck and shoulders. It had horns on its head—sometimes a single horn on its nose, sometimes a pair of horns over its eyes, or even horns on the shield. Every species was different.

|◀ Triceratops *is named after its three horns.*

A pair of horns at the top of the shield made the dinosaur look bigger and could cause deadly damage.

A broad shield covered the neck and shoulders.

The shield was brightly-colored to send warning signals to other animals.

Knobs and blades on the snout and above the eyes were used as battering rams.

Huge herds

Herds of ceratopsians grazed on the plains of
North America during the late Cretaceous period.
They kept to their own herds and could tell each other
apart by their horns. It is thought that the biggest male
ceratopsians had the biggest horns. These were used
for showing off and fighting to see who was going to
lead the herd and mate with the females.

Most dinosaur skulls are made of fragile bits of bone, so they are very rare. Ceratopsian skulls, however, are so solid they are quite common as fossils.

FACT

 If a meat-eater attacked, ceratopsians could defend themselves with their horns. They also may have used their neck shield and head horns to form a protective ring around the young if they were threatened by enemies.

Plated armor

One group of dinosaurs looked bigger and more threatening than many of the others. This is because they had a line of hard plates that stuck up along their backbone. These were the stegosaurs, or plated dinosaurs. *Stegosaurus* was the most famous of them all.

Plates and spikes

The *stegosaurs* had different arrangements of plates and spikes. Some dinosaurs had a lot of small plates. Some had only a few large plates. And some animals had spikes that covered the entire tail.

One of the last of the stegosaurs was the Chinese Wuerhosaurus. It had long, low plates.

The plates of Stegosaurus were probably covered in horn. They also may have been saw-edged to increase their effect as weapons.

Mysterious plates

There is still a lot experts do not know about the plated dinosaurs. Were the plates used for showing off? If so, they would be brightly-colored. If they absorbed the Sun's heat to keep the animal warm, then they would be covered in skin. Were they used for defense? If yes, they would have been covered in horn with sharp points and edges.

Armor in Action

Charging, ramming, pushing, and locking horns were some of the ways that armored dinosaurs battled each other and protected themselves from the meat-eaters.

Mighty battle

The impressive armor of the plant-eaters was not only used against meat-eating attackers, it also would have been used against one another. Dinosaurs fought each other for their position in the herd, just as modern herd animals do. The solid heads and the shoulder spikes of dinosaurs such as *Edmontonia* would have been used for battering, locking, and shoving.

An armor of broad plates lined the dinosaur's back.

The long, strong tail was also armor-plated.

Long spikes reached out from the shoulders.

Like a tank

Edmontonia and its relatives had backs covered in armor. They had backs that were covered in armor. Sheets of bony plates were embedded in the skin. These were covered in horn and had sharp points and edges. Deadly spines stuck out sideways and upward.

▶| Struthiosaurus *was the smallest of the armored dinosaurs.*

Bony eyelids protected the eyes.

The skull had bony plates fused to it.

A dangerous tail

To protect themselves against group attacks, many dinosaurs were armored from head to tail. One group of dinosaurs had a huge, heavy club at the end of a stiff tail. These dinosaurs used their strong hip muscles to swing the club at an attacker. Others had tails with sharp spikes.

⌃ Gastonia *was covered in spikes from its head to the tip of its tail. These razor-sharp spikes protected every part of its body against attackers.*

The last of the dinosaurs

The most famous of the tail-clubbed armored dinosaurs was *Ankylosaurus*. This creature lived during the Cretaceous period just as the plated dinosaurs began to die off. *Ankylosaurus* was one of the last dinosaurs to exist before these amazing creatures disappeared at the end of the Cretaceous period.

▶ Ankylosaurus *had thick, bony plates across its body. The end of its tail had a club, which was used to swing at enemies. The club was made up of bony knobs and could do a lot of damage.*

The Tiny Dinos

Not all of the dinosaurs were big and fierce. Some were small, graceful animals that were the ancestors of today's birds.

Feathers on the arms and on the legs helped *Microraptor* to glide.

Is it a bird? Is it a dinosaur?

Microraptor, the smallest dinosaur ever, was about the size of a crow. Feathers on the arms and legs helped *Microraptor* to glide. Other small dinosaurs were covered in feathers, too, but these were used for warmth rather than flight.

The feathered tail was used for steering.

Claws on the hands and feet allowed it to clamber through branches.

The gliding feathers on the arms and legs looked like four wings.

A handful of feathers

Protarchaeopteryx and *Caudipteryx* had a downy covering of feathers to help keep them warm, as well as bunches of feathers on their tail tips and forearms. The feathers on their forearms were probably used as nets for grabbing insects out of the air, or to help steady the animal as it ran.

Duck-sized Caudipteryx *and* Protachaeopteryx *shared the Cretaceous woodlands with early birds.*

Dinky dinosaurs

A tiny, early, armored dinosaur was *Scutellosaurus*, which was the size of a rabbit. It was covered by armor plates, which protected it from the larger dinosaurs that tried to bite it. One of the earliest dinosaurs found was also one of the smallest. *Compsognathus* was discovered in Germany in the 1850s. It was the size of a chicken and held the record of the smallest dinosaur until *Microraptor* was discovered in 2000.

Compsognathus *was built like the first bird,* Archaeopteryx. *They both lived at the same time and in the same place.*

Dinosaur fossils are still being found around the world by paleontologists. These are scientists who look for and study fossils of prehistoric animals and plants.

FACT

Tiny footprints and eggs

Fossils of dinosaur footprints, the size of those of a thrush, have been found in Novia Scotia. In Thailand, little dinosaur eggs, the size of a sparrow's eggs, have been discovered, but experts don't know what kind of dinosaur produced them. Finding the eggs proves that dinosaurs no bigger than small garden birds roamed Earth at the same time as the mighty giants.

Small is good

Fossils of dwarf dinosaurs, including sauropods, duckbills, and armored dinosaurs, have been found in some places. These dinosaurs were about the size of sheep. They probably lived on islands where there was not much food, so it was better to have a smaller body.

Scutellosaurus *lived in dangerous times with big meat-eaters like* Dilophosaurus *around.*

Eosipterus

The Dinosaur's World

When dinosaurs roamed the earth, it was a very different place from the world we know today. Strange-looking fish, mammals, and the first birds lived alongside the awesome dinosaurs.

Dinosaur killer

Not all dinosaur-age mammals were scuttling little animals that hid in the undergrowth. The spitting, snarling *Repenomamus* was about the size of a badger. It was the biggest dinosaur-age mammal that has ever been found. It was fierce and strong enough to eat dinosaurs such as *Psittacosaurus*.

baby *Psittacosaurus*

Confuciusornis

Xianglong

Repenomamus

Front teeth adapted
for nipping and
canines used for killing.

Short legs,
not built for
running.

Claws and
flat feet, like
a bear.

Hyphalosaurus

Flying reptiles

The pterosaurs were flying reptiles. There were two main types. The earlier ones had long tails and short wrists. The more advanced pterosaurs had short tails and long wrists and looked more like the birds we see today.

▼ Dimorphodon *was typical of the early pterosaurs. It had a long tail, short neck, and compact hands.*

Tools for the job

Some pterosaurs, like *Tapejara* that lived near lakes, had short, fruit-eating beaks. Others had comblike teeth for catching shrimp, or beaks and crushing jaws used for catching and eating shellfish. Fish-eating pterosaurs either had no teeth, or fish-trap snaggle teeth, like *Gallodactylus*. Some, like *Tropeognathus*, had blades that sliced through the water.

▶| *The biggest of the pterosaurs, such as* Quetzalcoatlus, *probably fed on fish or other animals that lived in the sea.*

FACTS

The later pterosaurs shared the skies with the first birds. They may have competed with one another for food, or have had different lifestyles but lived together, like birds and bats do today.

A sturdy wing

The wing of the pterosaur consisted of a sheet of membrane. This was supported by packs of gristly fibers that spread out from the arms and hand, in the same pattern as the flight feathers of a bird. There was also a flap of skin in the front of the arm that helped the pterosaur to move in different directions.

◄ The biggest pliosaurs, such as Liopleurodon, hunted the ichthyosaurs and other marine reptiles.

Fish reptiles

In dinosaur times, the seas were full of huge and strange-looking reptiles. The most highly adapted were the ichthyosaurs. They not only lived like dolphins, but also were shaped like dolphins. They even gave birth to live young at sea.

Sea monsters

The plesiosaurs were swimming reptiles with long necks. They swam slowly with turtlelike bodies and flippers, and snatched at fish with their toothy mouths. One group, the pliosaurs, were similar to the toothed whales of today.

Swimming lizards

Different types of sea creatures appeared at different periods. Placodonts were Triassic shellfish-eaters. Geosaurs were Jurassic marine crocodiles equipped with fins and flippers. Mosasaurs were giant swimming lizards from the Cretaceous period.

▽ *The big mosasaurs, such as* Tylosaurus, *hunted through the Cretaceous seas, as the pliosaurs did in Jurassic times.*

Timeline

Cretaceous period
144-65 million years ago

◄| *Velociraptor*

Jurassic period
213-144 million years ago

►| *Stegosaur*

◄| *Dilophosaurus*

Triassic period
248-213 million years ago

⊻ *Unaysaurus*

⊻ *Coelophysis*

◄ Tyrannosaurus rex

Other Cretaceous dinosaurs
- *Triceratops*
- *Giganotosaurus*
- *Suchomimus*
- *Masiakasaurus*
- *Nigersaurus*
- *Iguanodon*

◄ Ankylosaurus

Other Jurassic dinosaurs
- *Megalosaurus*
- *Dicraeosaurus*
- *Brachytrachelopan*
- *Ceratosaurus*

▼ Diplodocus

Other Triassic dinosaurs
- *Eoraptor*
- *Liliensternus*
- *Saturnalia*
- *Plateosaurus*
- *Melanorosaurus*

◄ Guaibasaurus

RECORD BREAKERS

Biggest plant-eater
Argentinosaurus, 115-130 feet (35-40 m) long; 80-100 metric tons (tonnes)

Biggest meat-eater
Giganotosaurus, 47 feet (14 m) long, 12 feet (4 m) tall, 8 tons (tonnes)

Tallest
Sauroposeidon, 60 feet (18 m) tall, more than 60 tons (tonnes)

Smallest
Microraptor, 16 inches (40 cm) long

Oldest
Eoraptor, about 230 million years old

Biggest skull
Pentaceratops, 9.8 feet (3 m) long

Most teeth
The plant-eating hadrosaurs had about 960 cheek teeth.

Longest neck
Sauroposeidon; its vertebrae (neck bones) were up to 4 feet (1.2 m) long.

Longest tail
Diplodocus, 43 feet (13 m) long.

Largest eggs
Hypselosaurus; a 100-million-year-old egg measures 1 foot (30 cm) long by 10 inches (25 cm) wide.

Shortest name
Minmi and *Khaan*

Longest name
Micropachycephalosaurus

Dinosaur Words

Pronunciation guide and meaning of names

Achelousaurus
ah-KELL-oo-SORE-us
Achelous: lizard (river god)

Allosaurus
AL-oh-SORE-us
other lizard

Ankylosaurus
an-KYE-loh-SORE-us
stiff lizard

Archaemphora (plants)
AHR-kee-EM-for-uh
ancient pitcher

Archaeopteryx
AHR-kee-OP-tuh-riks
ancient wing

Argentinosaurus
ahr-jen-TEEN-oh-SORE-us
Argentine lizard

Bambiraptor
BAM-bee-RAP-tore
small robber

Baryonyx
BARE-ee-ON-iks
heavy claw

Brachiosaurus
BRACK-ee-oh-SORE-us
arm lizard

Brachytrachelopan
BRAK-ee-TRAK-uh-LOH-pan
short-necked Pan (Greek god of pastures)

Caudipteryx
kawd-IP-ter-iks
tail feather

Centrosaurus
SEN-troh-SORE-us
pointed lizard

Ceratopsian
SEHR-uh-TOP-see-un
horn-faced

Ceratosaurus
seh-RAT-uh-SORE-us
horned lizard

Coelophysis
SEE-low-FYE-sis
hollow form

Compsognathus
komp-SOG-nuh-thus
pretty jaw

Confuciusornis
kun-FEW-shus-ORN-iss
Confucius bird

Coprolite
KOP-ruh-lite

Cretaceous
krih-TAY-shus

Deinonychus
dye-NON-ik-us
terrible claw

Dicraeosaurus
dye-KRAY-uh-SORE-us
two-forked lizard

Dilophosaurus
dye-LOH-fuh-SORE-us
two-ridged lizard

Dimorphodon
dye-MOR-foh-don
two-form tooth

Diplodocus
dih-PLOD-uh-kus
double beam

Edmontonia
ED-mon-TONE-ee-uh
from Edmonton in Canada

Edmontosaurus
ed-MON-toh-SORE-us
Edmonton lizard

Eoraptor
EE-oh-RAP-tor
early plunderer

Eosipterus
EE-oh-SIP-ter-us
dawn wing

Gallodactylus
GAL-oh-DAK-till-us
chicken fingers

Gastonia
gas-TONE-ee-uh
*named after fossil hunter
Robert Gaston*

Geosaur
JEE-oh-sore
rock lizard

Giganotosaurus
JIG-uhn-OH-toh-SORE-us
giant southern lizard

Guaibasaurus
GWYE-buh-SORE-us
Guaiba (Brazil) lizard

Hadrosaur
HAD-roh-sore
bulky lizard

Hyphalosaurus
HY-fall-oh-SORE-us
submerged lizard

Hypselosaurus
HIP-sih-luh-SORE-us
high-ridge lizard

Ichthyosaur
IK-thee-oh-SORE
fish lizard

Iguanodon
ig-WAH-nuh-don
iguana tooth

Jurassic
joo-RASS-ik

Kentrosaurus
KEN-troh-SORE-us
spur lizard

Khaan
kahn
ruler

Liliensternus
LIL-ee-en-STUR-nus
*named after paleontologist
Hugo Ruhle von Lilienstern*

Liopleurodon
LYE-oh-PLOOR-oh-don
smooth-sided tooth

Masiakasaurus
mah-SHEE-ah-kah-SORE-us
vicious lizard

Megalosaurus
MEG-uh-loh-SORE-us
great (huge) lizard

Melanorosaurus
MEL-uh-NOR-uh-SORE-us
black mountain lizard

Micropachysephalosaurus
MY-kroh-PAK-ee-SEF-uh-loh-SORE-us
tiny thick-headed lizard

Microraptor
MY-kroh-RAP-tor
small robber

Minmi
MIN-mee
*named after Minmi Crossing,
Queensland, Australia*

Mongolian
mong-GOHL-yuhn

Mosasaur
MOH-zuh-sore
river lizard

Nigersaurus
NEE-jer-SORE-us
Niger lizard after Niger in Africa

Ornithopod
OR-nith-uh-pod
bird foot

Paleontologist
PAY-lee-un-TAHL-uh-jist

Pangaea
pan-JEE-uh

Pentaceratops
PEN-tuh-SAYR-uh-tops
five-horned face

Placodont
PLAK-oh-dahnt
flat or plated teeth

Plateosaurus
PLAT-ee-oh-SORE-us
flat lizard

Plesiosaur
PLEE-zee-oh-sore
near lizard

Pliosaur
PLY-oh-SORE
greater lizard

Protarchaeopteryx
PROH-tar-kee-OP-ter-iks
early ancient wing

Protoceratops
PROH-toh-SAYR-uh-tops
first horned face

Psittacosaurus
SIT-uh-koh-SORE-us
parrot lizard

Pterosaur
TARE-uh-sore
winged lizard

Quetzalcoatlus
KET-zahl-koh-AT-lus
named for Aztec god Quetzalcoatl

Repenomamus
reh-PEN-oh-MAY-mus
reptile mammal

Saltasaurus
SALT-uh-SORE-us
lizard from Salta, Argentina

Saturnalia
sat-ur-NALE-yuh
festival of Saturn in ancient Rome

Sauropod
SORE-uh-pod
lizard foot

Sauroposeidon
SORE-oh-poh-SYE-duhn
lizard god of the sea

Scutellosaurus
skoo-TELL-oh-SORE-us
small shield lizard

Stegosaurus
STEG-uh-SORE-us
roof lizard

Struthiosaurus
STROOTH-ee-oh-SORE-us
ostrich lizard

Suchomimus
SOOK-oh-MIME-us
crocodile mimic

Tapejara
TAP-uh-JAR-uh
the old being

Triassic
try-a-sik

Triceratops
try-SAYR-uh-TOPS
three-horned face

Troodon
TROH-oh-don
wounding tooth

Tropeognathus
TROP-ee-OG-nah-thus
keel jaw

Tylosaurus
TYE-loh-SORE-us
swollen lizard

Tyrannosaurus
tye-RAN-uh-SORE-us
tyrant lizard

Unaysaurus
OO-nah-hee-SORE-us
Black water lizard (for region in Brazil)

Velociraptor
vel-OSS-ih-RAP-tor
quick plunderer

Xianglong
hung-lung
flying dragon (in Chinese)

Glossary

Carnivore An animal that eats other animals.

Coprolite Fossilized animal dung.

Down A fluffy, feathery covering on a bird or some dinosaurs, used to prevent heat loss.

Herbivore An animal that eats only plant material.

Mammal A warm-blooded animal that gives birth to live young and produces milk to feed them.

Pangaea The single supercontinent, formed of all the landmasses of the world, that broke up at the end of the Triassic period.

Prey An animal that is hunted by another.

Scavenger An animal that eats the flesh of something already dead.

Scute A bony plate that supports a covering of horn.

Index